Africa

In a faraway land
shaped just like
an elephant's ear,
families of elephants
roam the grasslands
of Kenya
at the foot of
Mt. Kilimanjaro.
This land is called Africa,
the kingdom
of the
elephants.

Library of Congress Cataloging-in-Publication Data Available

10 9 8 7 6 5 4 3 2 1

First paperback edition published in 2001 by
Sterling Publishing Company, Inc.
387 Park Avenue South, New York, N.Y. 10016
Distributed in Canada by Sterling Publishing
C/o Canadian Manda Group, One Atlantic Avenue, Suite 105
Toronto, Ontario, Canada M6K 3E7
Distributed in Great Britain and Europe by Chris Lloyd at
Orca Book Services, Stanley House, Fleets Lane
Poole BH15 3AJ, England.
Distributed in Australia by Capricorn Link (Australia) Pty. Ltd.
P.O. Box 704, Windsor, NSW 2756 Australia

Printed and Bound in China

Sterling ISBN 0-8069-2098-X Trade
         0-8069-2095-5 Paper

Produced by Discovery Channel Publishing
Copyright © 1998 by Discovery Communications, Inc.
Photographs by Karl Ammann © Discovery Communications, Inc.,
Except: pages 9, 19, and 34-35 © Karl Ammann;
pages 12, 16, 17, 18, 22, 28, 32, 36, 37, 39, 40, 41, 43 and 45 from the
film *Africa's Elephant Kingdom* © Discovery Communications, Inc.;
page 20 © Charles Freligh.
Art Direction and Illustration by Deborah Orbell Freligh.

Discovery Communications, Inc., brings understanding to new levels
through the highest quality nonfiction television programming, publishing
and film production. *Little Bull: Growing Up in Africa's Elephant Kingdom*
is inspired by *Africa's Elephant Kingdom*, a large-format film produced by
Discovery Channel Pictures. Discovery Networks, a division of
Discovery Communications, Inc., operates Discovery Channel,
TLC (The Learning Channel), Animal Planet and Travel Channel.
Visit their website at http://www.discovery.com/

For Carrie, Caty, and Will

Little Bull

GROWING UP IN AFRICA'S ELEPHANT KINGDOM

 Discovery KIDS™ ELLEN FOLEY JAMES

STERLING PUBLISHING, NEW YORK

EARLY ONE MORNING,

as the rising sun spread its
light across the wide African sky,
a baby elephant was born.

His name was Little Bull.

Wrapped like a cabbage in his big elephant ears,
Little Bull lay very still.
His grassy bed was soft and damp from weeks of rain.

Little Bull lifted one ear and listened.
The very first thing he heard was
the bright chatter of birds.

The very first thing he smelled was the warm, wet grass.

And the very first
thing he felt
was his mother's
long, wiggly trunk
gently nudging
him to stand.

This was not so easy for a newborn baby elephant.
From the tip of his trunk to the tuft of his tail,
Little Bull weighed two hundred and fifty pounds!

But soon he was up,
stumbling and swaying on his wobbly legs.
From the bottom of his toes to the top
of his ears, he stood three feet tall.

Now he could reach
his mother's side
and the warm place
where he rested his
cheek while he
drank her milk.

Little Bull lived with his family on the grassy plains of Africa.

His playground was all the outdoors, as far as he could see,
a land of rolling hills and umbrella trees. And in the distance,
rising up like the slope of an elephant's back,
was the great White Mountain.

In Little Bull's family there were
mothers and grandmothers, aunts and cousins,
sisters and brothers and babies.
Grandmother Torn Ear was the
oldest and wisest in the group.
She knew how to protect her family from danger.
And from all her
wandering over the years,
she remembered where to find
the watering holes and sweet leaves
and green grass to eat.

Little Bull's favorite toy was his own wriggly trunk. Grasping for stones, picking up sticks, he waved it and wiggled it and taught himself tricks.

Little Bull's
mother showed
him how to lift
his trunk to sniff
the air for
strange new smells.
He put it
in her mouth
to say
"Hello,"
and curled it
around her tusk
to say,
"Let's play."

Little Bull's favorite friend was his baby girl cousin, Keekay.
They wrestled and tumbled and tangled their trunks while
the grownups stood about and swished their tails.

Sometimes, when his mother was busy with the grownups, Little Bull tried standing on his head to get her attention.

His humpty-dumpty body toppled over every time.

Little Bull's family went everywhere together,
and Little Bull was never lonely.
The older cousins huddled close to the little ones to
keep them out of trouble.

But Little Bull was especially curious, so his big sister
kept a watchful eye on him while he explored.
He liked to chase the egrets, who joined the group
like party guests whenever the elephants stopped to rest.

Other
strange creatures
came to the
marshes
to drink
with Little Bull
and his family.
There were
zebras with
wavy stripes
and ears
that twitched.

There were cranes with fancy feathers and legs as skinny as sticks.

Sometimes there was danger hiding nearby.
One day, peeking out from behind his mother's legs,
Little Bull saw six bright eyes staring at him.

All at once, he heard a cry like a wild trumpet from
Grandmother Torn Ear. The big elephants rushed
around Little Bull in a cloud of dust.
Safe inside a circle of legs and tails and tusks,
he watched the bright-eyed lions bound away.

That evening, Little Bull saw a huge, dark mountain
moving across the plain. It was Old Bull, Little Bull's father.
He stood in the shadows all night long. By morning he was gone.

The days grew hot and dry. No rain had fallen for weeks.
The grass was dying and the rivers were drying up.
The elephants walked for miles along the dusty plains,
searching for anything to eat or drink.

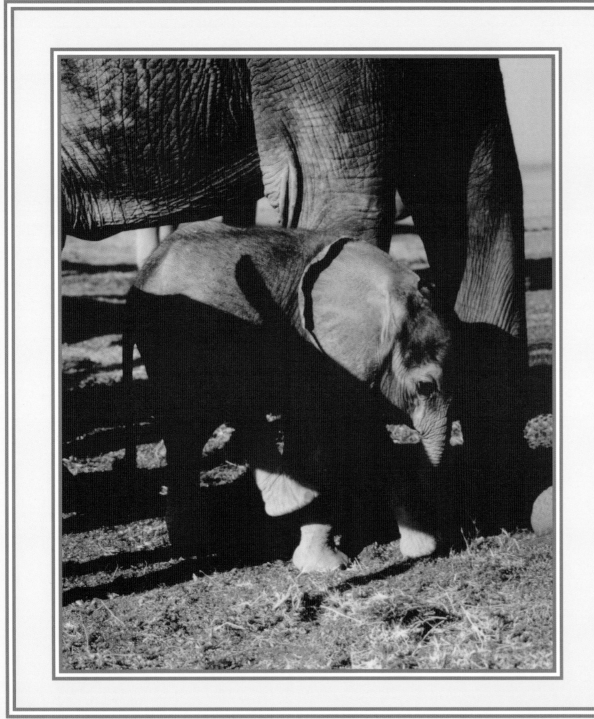

Little Bull
was hungry
and thirsty
and tired.
When the family
stopped to rest,
he tucked
himself into
a cool, shady spot
between
his mother's
legs.

The older
elephants stood
in the hot sun,
pulling up twigs
and thorns
and dusty
brown grass.

Where was
the rain?

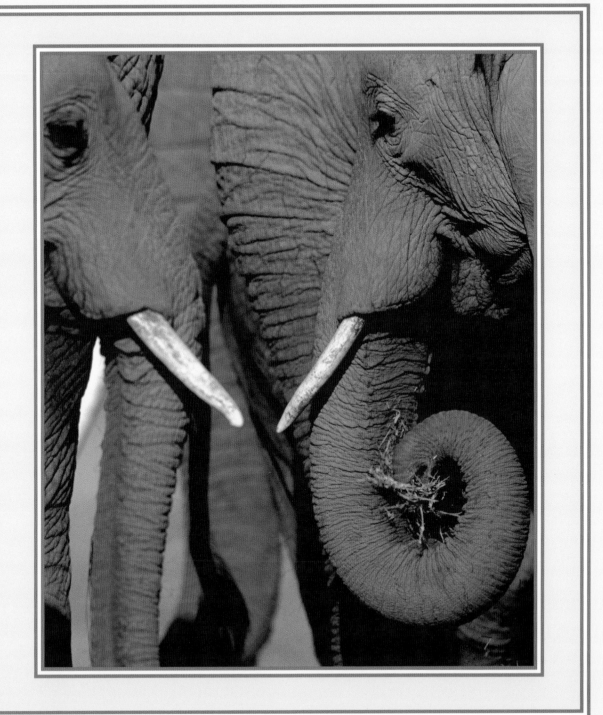

At night, Little Bull slept.
The ground beneath him made a very hard bed.
The sky was a bowl of bright stars overhead,
without a single cloud or even a hint of rain.

During the long journey to find food,
Little Bull hurried to follow his mother's tail.
He tried to stay in her shadow,
out of the burning sun.
But his little legs had to work twice as hard to keep up.

Keekay was
the smallest
baby in
the family.
Every time
she stumbled,
her mother
slowed down
to wait
for her.

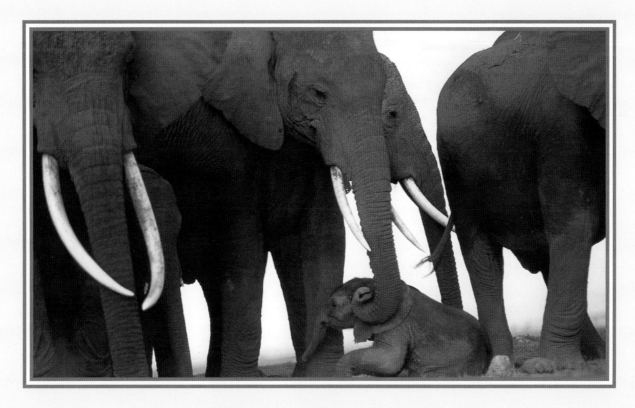

With so little to eat,
Keekay was too weak to play with Little Bull.
Sometimes, after her nap, she was too tired to walk.
The other elephants stroked her softly with their trunks
and nudged her to stand.

The dry season went on and on.
Little Bull forgot that he had ever heard
the sound of raindrops.
He forgot that he had ever seen
green grass or splashed in muddy puddles.
Every day there was less and less
of his mother's warm, sweet milk to drink.

One afternoon, Little Bull lifted his trunk
toward the smell of wet earth in the distance.
All the elephants turned their ears toward the thunder.
Dark clouds rolled across the sky, bringing the delicious rains.

The rain soaked
the ground
and fed the dry grass
and filled the water holes
to overflowing.

Little Bull felt
the sharp, fresh
wind next to
his skin.
He wanted to play.
When he raised
his trunk toward
his mother,
a tiny white tusk
poked out of
his mouth like
a baby's
new tooth.

Little Bull and his family waded into the swamps and wallowed and splashed in the cool mud.

At last there was plenty of water to drink and new grass to eat.

In just a few days, Keekay was strong enough to romp in the muddy swamp with her mother.

Soon everything was green again.
Little Bull and his sisters and brothers and cousins
chased each other in the tall grass until the sun went down.

One bright morning,
Little Bull found
an old playmate
waiting for him.

He remembered when
the egrets had flocked around
his family before the long
dry season. Now they, too,
had returned with the rain.

As he grew, Little Bull remembered where he had been and what he had seen. One day his memories would make him wise, like his grandmother.

One day,
like his father,
Little Bull would leave
his family to find his own way.

And the wide African sky would watch over him.

Glossary

AFRICA: The second largest continent in the world, Africa is home to more than 600 million people. Fewer than 600,000 elephants roam Africa today, primarily on the grassy plains of central and southern Africa.

CRANE: A tall wading bird that lives in marshes and on plains. It feeds on grains and small animals.

DRY SEASON: A time of the year when no rain falls and the grasslands of Africa dry out. This season is followed by a period of heavy rainfall, which brings plants back to life.

EGRET: A small, white bird that has long legs, a long neck, and a slender body. Egrets live in swamps, marshes, and rivers, where they wade to catch fish in their beaks.

ELEPHANT: The African elephant is the largest land mammal in the world. An adult can grow to be up to ten feet tall and can weigh 12,000 pounds. Elephants have large ears, thick skin, and long trunks. Adult elephants usually have tusks.

GRASSLAND: A flat plain covered with grass and a few trees and bushes. African grasslands are home to such animals as zebras, elephants, and antelopes. Heavy summer rains and thunderstorms help plants to grow there. These are an important food source for many animals.

LION: A large, meat-eating member of the cat family found in the grasslands of Africa. Lions hunt in small family groups called prides. They are golden yellow and can weigh up to 520 pounds. Male lions have thick manes.

SWAMP: A low, wet area with trees and grasses.

TRUNK: The nose and upper lip of an elephant. An elephant trunk can weigh up to 300 pounds and can hold up to two gallons of water. It can be used for eating, washing, smelling, lifting, communicating, and sometimes for fighting.

TUSK: A long elephant tooth made of ivory that elephants use for protection and as a tool for digging and stripping bark from trees. Tusks are also considered status symbols within the herd. A tusk grows about seven inches each year throughout an elephant's life and can weigh as much as 200 pounds.

UMBRELLA TREE: Also known as an acacia tree, this evergreen is often found in tropical regions of Africa. Its leaves provide shade to many animals.

WATER HOLE: A low point in the ground that fills with rain during the wet season. Animals gather there to find water to drink. Even holes created by elephant feet that fill with water are considered water holes for small animals.

WHITE MOUNTAIN: Also known as Mount Kilimanjaro, it is the highest mountain in Africa. The mountain is a volcano that is now extinct.

ZEBRA: A horse-like mammal with distinctive black and white stripes. Zebras usually travel in herds.

Index

AFRICA 1, 4, 10, 47

CRANE 21

EGRET 19, 42, 43

GRASSLAND 1, 10

LION 22, 23

SWAMP 39, 40

TRUNK 7, 8, 14-16, 33, 36, 38

TUSK 15, 23, 38

UMBRELLA TREE 5, 10-11

WATER HOLE 13, 37

WHITE MOUNTAIN 11

ZEBRA 20